HOW
TO MAKE A WOMAN HAPPY
A GUIDE FOR MEN

Denis Hickey

If you let your love down, it dies.

Published by Vingdinger Publishing LLC
Copyright © Denis Hickey 2014

ISBN (paperback): 978-0-9888588-6-2
ISBN (e-book): 978-0-9888588-5-5
Library of Congress Control Number: 2014920940

Book design by Kazimierz Pelczar
Editing by Jill Ronsley
E-book formatting by Sun Editing & Book Design

Websites:
denishickey.com
breakingfree-thebooks.com

Printed and bound in the USA

Dedicated to the women
who have enhanced my life

Aurianne Jacobs
Aneta Struk
Audriel Hinds
Aunt Gussie
Aunt Floss
Bridget Harris
Carolyn Guidry
Carole Wiegardt
Carol
Chimene Hickey
Diane Huntsberger
Dolly O'Connell
Donna Joyce
Donna and Elizabeth Sussman
Ella Hinds (in memory)
Ellen and Jilli Joss
Elise Rousseau
Ewa Rau
Eve and Patty Flynn
Ewa and Zosia Woznicka
Hannie Kapka
Franci Stagi
Jan and Ellen Beth Grossnickle
Janet Webber
Janet (Seph) Winslow
Jill Ronsley
Jinny Jones
Jackie Hanna
Jody Love
Jordan Duval

Joy Makno
Jowita Waniek
Judy Blades
Julia Schmidt
Julie, Carol, and Deanna Zolfo
Kathleen Hickey
Kathryn Hickey
Kathy and Tiffany Laton
Kay Eastwood
Laura Ghiron
Laurel Garceau
Lynn Colman
Lynn Keeley
Maddie Zolfo
Maddie Gunders, Debbi Ryan,
    Dana Gunders
Malgosia Woznicka-Hickey
Mami Sinclair
Marilyn O'Connell
Mary, Anne Marie and Ruth
    Chanecka
Nicola Disko, Gudrun Disko
Pam Slater
Patricia Berryhill
Sandy Dutra
Shannon Hickey
Sharon Colman
Terry Henry
Virginia Colman
Zosia Fleming

Acknowledgements

I would like to acknowledge Clive Matson and members of his writing sessions, who worked with me to think this book through; Rob and Rich, who contributed ideas; the many men and women over the years who told me of their experiences; Shannon, for her editing; my wife, Malgosia, for the practice and website. Thanks to my editor, Jill Ronsley, for her editing, advice, publishing expertise and positive attitude. A special thanks to Kazimierz Pelczar for the artwork, interior design, covers and general advice.

About the Author

Denis Hickey grew up in a family headed by strong, loving women who provided him with a sound basis to write this book. He ran his first business at twenty-six and retired at forty-eight to backpack around the world and write. In between he raised a fun family with a wonderful woman and two lovely daughters, Shannon and Chimene. In business he learned entrepreneurial skills in Silicon Valley and worked with companies on the leading edge of five different technologies. Later he co-founded the crisis management firm, Hickey & Hill.

Denis lives in Warsaw, Poland, with his second wife, Malgosia, and son, Sean, pursuing his passion for writing and striving to achieve a mellow satisfaction in life.

Other books by Denis Hickey, published by
Vingdinger Publishing:
The Breaking Free Series:
Breaking Free (Book 1)
The Traveler (Book 2)

denishickey.com
breakingfree-thebooks.com

Table of Contents

Introduction 1
Feel in Your Bones! 3

THE BASICS **5**
Fun Is Living in the Moment 6
Affection Is Cool 7
"Pay Me a Compliment, Melvin!" 14
 Practice Being Romantic : Mood, Ideas, Easy Recipes 18
Communication Skills for the "Impaired" 25
Change One Thing for Her 29
Traditions: Keeping Romance Alive 31

GIFT-GIVING AND GIFT IDEAS **38**
Gift-Giving Occasions 41
The Big 3 41
Mother's Day 45
No-Special-Occasion-Whatsoever Occasion 46
Tough Guy Gifts 48
"Keep Her Happy" Cheat Sheet 49

SPECIAL ISSUES **53**
Removing Roadblocks to Her Happiness 55
Reactivating Long-Term Relationships 62
Fixing What Is Broken 67

BECOMING A MAN WHO MAKES WOMEN HAPPY **73**

ATTACHMENTS **77**
"Romance" Cheat Sheet 79
Elaborate Menu for the Advanced 81
"Keep Her Happy" Cheat Sheet 85

Introduction

This handbook is dedicated to the premise that men want to make women happy, and that with a few suggestions, some informed effort, and the judicious engaging and disengaging of the ego, we can learn to do it better, improve our relationships, and make our own lives happier. (Warning: Consistent use of ideas contained in this guide may inundate you with interesting, loving, intelligent, desiring, loyal and happy women.)

Several years ago, my friend Rich Rawley approached me with the idea of writing a book for men about how to make a woman happy. Rich is a man who makes his woman happy. I have observed their interplay as a couple, and I can attest that during the twenty years I've known him, Rich always has good things to say about his beloved.

When Rich suggested the idea, I immediately recalled a conversation I'd had with a twenty-something cabbie in Chicago years earlier. I was his last customer for the night, and he told me that after he dropped me off he was going to his girlfriend's place. I took the liberty of asking a few questions and got him to describe his anticipated evening with his girlfriend. Without going into detail, I can say that what he described demonstrated such cluelessness that I finally said, "Hey, you can't do that!"

"Why not?" he asked.

"Because one thing you want in a relationship is respect, and your approach sounds anything but respectful."

To my surprise, he was curious about my comment. He said he didn't know much about women, and asked for advice. I gave him an idea or two that had worked for me in the past. After the cabbie dropped me off, I wondered how many men were that clueless about women.

Rich's idea appealed to me. I was fortunate in life to have women of strong character help develop my thought process and ease with other women. It seemed fitting to pass on lessons I learned to those less fortunate than me, and to pay tribute to the many women that have enriched my life to which I have dedicated this book.

Rich Rawley has been kind enough to contribute two chapters and stories. Although we are not certified experts, we have learned through time and experience what pleases women and what's simply clueless. I have also talked to numerous women and men over the years, individually and in discussion groups, about the subject of how men can make women happy.

This book is not about saving relationships that are fatally flawed. It is about taking relationships that are new, okay, not bad, doing fine, getting old or facing trouble and making them exhilarating, exciting or just plain workable. It was written for men who want ideas. Sometimes one idea is all you need–and this book offers ideas aplenty.

About the title: Of course people generally have to make themselves happy. Women can certainly be happy (or unhappy) through their work, the joy of their children, their creativity, exchange of ideas, travel, art, whatever. But there is something in men intrinsically, a primitive urge perhaps, that drives us to want to make women happy. How often have you said or heard this male refrain: "I was just trying to make her happy!"

Feel in Your Bones!

Women deserve happiness. Think about it! Check out how much women care for us by handling the bulk of the family chores we are indifferent to. They maintain social contact with family and friends, because we are not so inclined. They manage doctors' appointments, remember shoe sizes, shop for clothing, attend school meetings, know what to bring to a party, feed the kids and often do the family accounting and pay bills even when they earn the highest wage in the family.

And how about care-giving? Some years ago, my friend Susan invited me to her uncle's house for dinner. When I got there, she and her two cousins were feeding their feeble Uncle Jim, whose life was clearly ebbing away. In a kitchen chair rigged to keep him from falling out, Jim sat slumped forward and barely moving. Incomprehensible speech dribbled from his mouth along with mashed potatoes and spinach. The ladies somehow understood his wishes and tended to him as they chatted to each other about family dynamics.

Don't they give us sympathy when we are down? Don't they give us an ear to bend in triumph or in friendship, when we feel the need to bleed our souls? Picture in your mind the positive emotion they elicit from us, such as when they dance or make us laugh. There's no doubt that women make our lives vibrant and thrilling–so much so that if our woman were seriously threatened, we would die for her.

You can crow about the ultimate thrills found in business conquests, or jumping out of planes, or deep diving to glimpse spectacular fish and ocean life, but for most of us guys the sheer intensity of intimacy and sexual pleasure with a woman is the most electrifying single event we will ever experience. Just watching my lady sway inside her dress gives me a thrill.

Who takes away our loneliness? Who makes our holidays sweet? And, when you take time to think about it, what is sweeter than a woman's laughter or enthusiasm, more alluring than her pride, more touching than her tenderness, more provocative than her skirt blowing in the breeze or more intimate than a smile meant just for you? Don't your thoughts of happiness almost always include a woman–as she watches the sun set, plays with your hair like found treasure or lights up while unwrapping a gift you've given her? And then, when life has torn you down, Mom is on the phone. "Oh hello, dear! I was just thinking of you."

You get the picture. If you can't say that one woman you know deserves happiness, you are truly dead. Now, close your eyes and try to feel this sentiment:

 **!important:**
Your mother, sister, cousin, aunt, friend, lover or the woman at the grocery store deserves happiness!

THE BASICS

Fun Is Living in the Moment

Women like a man who is fun, and fun is in the moment. "In the moment" means being able to put aside chores, phones, computers, responsibilities and thoughts of past and future. It is about what is happening now. "In the moment" is good sex, the thrill of your first base hit or basket or goal, your first kiss, the day you fell in love, movies and popcorn, connecting with someone. "In the moment" you feel what is around you, like textures and emotions. You have time to see people's facial expressions and physical actions. You have time to empathize and to laugh. A recent study found that 73% of women are attracted to a man with a sense of humor.

Suggestion:
Be with her in the moment. *Decide that you are not in a hurry. Breathe in deeply, and on the exhale pay attention to your surroundings. Smell, see, hear …*

Affection Is Cool

Webster's *New Encyclopedic Dictionary* defines affection very simply: a "tender feeling of attachment, fondness …" Simplicity fits, because affection seems simple when it is received, doesn't it? It feels like a warm, lazy summer day with a cold beer close by. With practice affection is comfortable and easy to apply. Almost any pet dog can give people tail-wagging affection that lets us know we are important. If a dog can do it, we certainly can!

The characteristics women have told me they love about men include being reliable, generous, stable, tender, compassionate, playful and adaptable; they should be a good lover and a loving father; they should be able to give reassurance and a secure, warm hug. These qualities can be called upon to give the gift of affection.

And don't even think about affection not being manly! John Wayne, Harrison Ford and Russell Crowe are just three men who mastered the art of being affectionate and rugged at the same time.

Story: My action hero is my boyhood friend, John Flynn, a six-foot five-inch, 240-pound New York cop. He worked in Emergency Services. That meant he and his partner drove around in a specially outfitted truck geared to handle unusual circumstances, like pulling people out of car wrecks, dismantling bombs or, if someone happened to drive off a pier into the water, diving in after them. One night when he was off duty, John was summoned to rescue three painters, marooned and unconscious inside a mammoth circular water tank perched on top of iron stilts three hundred feet in the air. The painters had apparently removed their gas masks while painting the inside of the tank, and had become disoriented and asphyxiated.

In the middle of a raging Long Island storm, John was lowered into the tank in a makeshift seat for one person. He said the immensity inside the white cylinder made him feel like he was in the middle of a snowy whiteout in the Alps. Standing at the bottom of the tank, John bundled up two of the unresponsive painters and lowered them through piping that fed down to ground level and the waiting ambulances. He attached the third man to his rigging, unstrapped his own oxygen mask and placed it over the unconscious guy's mouth. Then John grabbed onto the rigging, motioned the rescuers to begin hoisting them up, and hung on. During the lift to safety he struggled desperately to maintain consciousness. In the end, just one of the three painters survived.

On a TV talk show shortly after the incident, when John was asked how he felt about being branded a hero, he said, "The hero is my wife, Eve. I'm just doing my job. She's the one who has to worry and wait up for me to come home. She's the real hero." It may seem like a cliché to some people, but John meant every word.

 **Tips for You:**

☛ Appreciation and support are charms. Tell her how much you appreciate her organizing your birthday party, how nice the shirt she ironed looks and how intelligent she is. If she brings in the bucks, definitely appreciate that. Affection and appreciation are partners.

☛ What better way to show affection than being genuinely happy to see her? Imagine how she would feel–how anyone would feel–knowing that they were important and wanted.

☛ Make an extra effort to notice her. How about leaving easy-to-find love or appreciation notes around the house or sending the same sort of text messages? A warm smile works; so does putting your hand over hers, or your arm around her with a gentle squeeze on her shoulder, or asking her advice. She may be shocked at first, but hey, you are in the middle of change. Right?

☛ Compliments are often affectionate.

☛ Asking her what she thinks would be affectionate.

☛ **Affection is best when it is subtle.**

 **Story:** *A while back, I had business with a farmer in Northern California. He was a big, burly man of sixty-five, with sledgehammer wrists. He talked like a backwoodsman but was smart like a fox. Andy owned large tracts of rice, row crops and timberland. During our dinner discussions, he would often tell me about*

his wife of forty years. He said she would go with him on weekly drive-through of his agricultural properties, at night when the moon was bright and things were quiet. I mentioned that he seemed to have a devoted relationship with his wife and asked for any words of wisdom he might be willing to impart. He said, in his gruff way, "Well, I'll tells ya, you treat a woman good–and she treats you great!"

When I got back from my trip, I brought flowers to my wife, using the "Guess which hand behind my back" approach. She broke into an easy smile that said, my hero! That night I got a great massage.

No need to go overboard. For Andy, a man who keeps his emotions severely constrained, I'm sure asking his wife to drive with him showed a lot of unspoken but clearly communicated affection.

Tried and True

The pat. Many men probably like to give the old pat on the butt, possibly derived from similar manly pats on the basketball court or football field. Let's face it, the affectionate pat on our woman's butt–not to be confused with the potentially explosive pat on someone else's–is a favorite way for us to show affection. Don't overuse it! Check her body language. "Ouch," a wince or the words "Stop that!" means you have transgressed. You should know when she doesn't like it, just as you should know when a kid doesn't like to be tickled. Facial expressions make it obvious. Handled properly, however, a little pat on the ass once in a while can be affectionate. Even if she doesn't seem to notice, you lose something when you stop.

The hug. Like any art, touching needs practice. Some people like hugs, some are uncomfortable with them. Some people never learn how to hug.

Story: *A friend–I'll call him George–divorced and then remarried a few years later. George invited me to dinner along with a member of his old family (his twenty-two-year-old daughter, Jill) and the entire new family (George's current wife and her two college-age kids). The dinner wasn't pleasant. We sat around a kitchen table loaded with London broil, corn on the cob, Caesar salad and baked potatoes. Tension filled the air. Jill exuded an angry possessiveness, which mixed dangerously with the possessiveness of the college kids and nearly negated the savory aroma of the London broil.*

During the meal, Jill butted heads with her father's new family. I had known her for a long time, and after dinner I took her to a local bar for a beer and some conversation. She told me horrible things about her father that related to her parents' breakup, and then let me play devil's advocate long enough for me to get across the reason why her dad was my friend. When she had cooled down a bit, I asked what else was under the surface of her anger. She sipped her beer, then broke down and cried, "He doesn't love me! He never hugs me. Never hugs or touches any of his real kids."

During the ensuing discussion about her father's family's hugging habits, she revealed that her paternal grandmother was a "cold fish." She said she'd never seen her grandmother, or for that matter the more respected grandfather, touch either their son (Jill's father) or any of their grandchildren. A light switched on in my head. Other than giving a vigorous handshake, George shied away from touching me as well. Eventually, Jill and I concluded that her father had never been taught to hug.

The next day, I wrote George a letter about our conversation. But, after considering the pros and cons, I decided to withhold it from him. A couple of years later, I was enjoying a pina colada while relaxing in a lounge chair on the superbly manicured lawn in George's backyard. The second drink gave me the courage to tell George about the letter, which I still had with me. He asked to read it. Then he paused, speechless. During that pause, incredibly, Jill stopped by to say hello. George stood up, walked towards her and enfolded her in a hug. I was uncomfortable watching. He seemed like a knight in a suit of armor, gallant but oh, so stiff. However, although it was awkward, both he and his daughter appeared to be pleased with the effort.

The point is: it's never too late to learn to hug–especially since hugs are now fashionable for men.

Warning: You can feel by a person's body language if he or she is comfortable being hugged. If you feel stiffness, or they pull away, or you notice anguish in their eyes, back off! If it's a first-meeting hug, make it short, or pass it up and practice with family members and people you know.

The tap. Last year I watched the video of my second wedding. During the lineup to greet the bride and groom, my friend Christian tapped the side of my face with a look that said, "I am happy for you, my buddy." It's been eleven years since the wedding and I can instantly recall his affection for me that day. Just a tap! Now I also use the "tap."

But be careful–a tap too hard is a slap.

Use at any age! Affection doesn't take notice of age.

Story: *Several years ago I was in Cambodia, dining in an outdoor restaurant on the Gulf of Thailand's golden shores. I saw a Western man in his mid-seventies sitting with an attractive, petite Cambodian woman around age twenty-two. The man's body motions and the type of eyeglasses he wore reminded me of my Uncle Lon, whom I revered. I stole glimpses of the couple. They obviously had genuine fondness for each other. You could tell by the way her brown eyes sparkled when she smiled, the way her body moved towards him, sweet and loving, and the affection in the way he spoke, though his words were sparing and he held himself somewhat stiffly. I don't know what their connection was, but between them I saw a beauty as elegant as any artistic offering.*

Danger. Criticism can be given with love, affection and a genuine wish for a person's well-being. On the other hand, constant criticism (how she dresses, her weight, her family, cleanliness of the home, etc.) can turn statements like "I will love you forever," "You make me feel…" and "You fill me up …" into "You've lost that loving feeling." Constant criticism is lethal to relationships and the antithesis of affection. Conversely, affection goes a long way towards restoring that loving feeling with the woman in your life or warmth between family members and friends.

Practice random acts of affection.

"Pay Me a Compliment, Melvin!"

Story: *"Pay me a compliment, Melvin!" said Helen Hunt to Jack Nicholson in the movie As Good As It Gets. "I need one, quick. You have no idea how much you hurt my feelings." Hunt's character, Carol, was expressing her anger after she had dressed up carefully for an evening of dinner and dancing, only to have Melvin say, "I don't get it. They make me wear a jacket and they let you in wearing a housedress." Now she stared sullenly into Melvin's eyes and educated him, "A compliment is something nice about someone else."*

Melvin fumbled around for a compliment, finally telling her that he had been reluctant to take the pills he had been prescribed for his various phobias, but after meeting her he had started taking the pills. His eyebrows arched with sincerity. "My compliment is," he said, "you make me want to be a better man."

A sense of pride flowed like a wave across Carol's face. She leveled a trusting smile at him and said, "That may be the best compliment of my life."

Compliment a woman's intelligence, her looks, her dress, her scent. There is something flattering to say about most women.

Try these:
- "That's fascinating! Tell me more."
- "I like your hair."
- "Nice blouse!"
- "Sometimes I just like to look at you."
- For a girlfriend or wife, there is always the magnificence of her breasts, to be savored with awe: "Oh, my God! I am so lucky. You are a goddess, baby!"
- Tantalizing scents may waft through the air: "Wow! I like your perfume!"
- How about taste? "What did you put in that soup? It tastes wonderful!" (Simple is good here).

It's not so much what you say, so you don't have to be cute. It's simply that you noticed. How often do you hear a man complimenting a female family member, friend, casual acquaintance or fellow worker? It happens with the frequency of becoming a lottery winner. Let's face it, not much is expected of us men regarding compliments, so when we do connect it is definitely appreciated. Giving compliments is like picking low-hanging apples in the orchard. Compliments are gifts that take less time than walking to the kitchen for a beer. But they set you apart from other men.

In years past, it was a gentlemanly art to notice and comment. Learn to give compliments naturally. You'll get better with practice, and the rewards will be high.

Story: I grew up in a female-dominated family. My grandmother, whom we called Ahma, was the matriarch. Five-foot-one, she wore high heels and moved fast. Her passion made her *seem bigger than life. Ahma's jet-black hair was always bunched in curls at the top of her head, supported in back by one of her many enormous Spanish latticework combs with tooth-like daggers. My brothers and I loved to make her happy. We'd say things like, "That color looks good on you, Ahma," or "Your eyes are really sparkling today," which was usually true. Vanity was her middle name, and the surefire way to get her in a good mood, would be to say, "How old are you Ahma? Forty-five?" When she'd giggle and respond, "Never ask a lady her age," we really poured it on. "I'm serious, Ahma! I hope I look that young at forty." It became natural for me to compliment her.*

While simple flattery worked well for Ahma, compliments about personality, skill or intelligence, were more appropriate for my mother and aunts. You need to be able to add subtle twists for different people. The amazing thing is that for many years I never realized my talent for the art of flattery, even though there were always a lot of women in my life who liked me.

Use Common Sense. There are pitfalls on the way to mastering this particular art, to be sure. You may encounter obstacles and boundaries that invite misinterpretation. For instance, it's generally not a good idea to give a woman a compliment while you're staring at her breasts (unless the situation is one in which you intentionally want to compliment her breasts). That can be dangerous–like starting a conversation in the urinal with a guy you don't know well, while staring at his dick. And be careful not to confuse a compliment with an advance. Nearly every woman has had the experience of fending off some dork who simply cannot be educated about the fact that she does not want him to pursue her. To some men, the concept of boundaries is rocket science.

Story: My friend Patricia told me about how her boss would complement her while chasing her around his shop after closing time. She quit. It wasn't that she didn't like him—she didn't like the chase. She tried to signal this gracefully, but his antennae never picked up the signal. His advances, as cute as he thought they were, were harassment that forced Patricia to leave a job she otherwise liked.

Stories like Patricia's probably scare a lot of well-intentioned men away from giving compliments. They are afraid to say the wrong thing for fear of an adverse reaction. In his book *Blink: The Power of Thinking without Thinking*, Malcolm Gladwell says that making snap judgments about someone is part of the makeup of human beings, allowing us to make quick assessments about whether someone is friendly or hostile, but that with education and experience these instincts become better able to judge reality. In other words, practice makes perfect.

How can a man know what is okay to compliment, and when?

Tips:
- Every chance you get, watch how women notice a compliment. Observe their reactions to judge what to say and when. Then practice.

- ☞ Remember that common sense and sincerity always make a good impression.
- ☞ Be careful not to use compliments too effusively.
- ☞ Think about what you really like about her, or what she does to make you proud.
- ☞ Get in the habit of the occasional compliment. Appreciate her competence and skills, body, face or dress. **Avoid** complimenting while your mind is working over her body.
- ☞ Let a compliment stand for what it is–a random gift.

Story: *In the coffee shop of the Bristol Hotel in Warsaw, an elegantly dressed older woman was having cappuccino and cherry cobbler with a well-dressed man her age, possibly her husband. She had a charming smile. Suddenly, a much younger man in sweatpants walked over to their table and, excusing himself to her companion, looked into her eyes and said, "I've been sitting over by the window and couldn't help notice your beautiful smile." He turned to the companion. "You are a lucky man." Then he walked away. The woman glowed, and you can bet her companion was proud.*

Moral: Age doesn't matter.

Practice Being Romantic

Danielle Steel is a gazillionaire because so many women love romance novels. They want to be swept away by an adventurous, intelligent, witty, attractive person. We all need a little razzle-dazzle to spice up our humdrum lives. Yet, for whatever reason, maybe because we're shy or lazy, many of us prefer to veg out on the couch watching TV action heroes capture her heart. Why get upstaged? Be that romantic person once in a while. You can be romantic without spending a lot of money. Switch into the moment and cook up something special for someone special.

Ingredients:

- ✓ Find out what is romantic to her.
- ✓ Plan ahead.
- ✓ Initiate action.
- ✓ Set the mood.
- ✓ Practice! Practice! Practice!

Start by finding out what is romantic to her. Ask her! Otherwise, you may just be romancing yourself. If your relationship is new or she doesn't know how to answer your question, check out how she reacts to whatever you conjure up.

 **Tips**:

- ☛ **Be loving.** This could be through a card, an e-mail or a text message containing a love poem or simple statement saying that you love or appreciate her. I've just sent my love an e-mail that took fifteen seconds to compose. Don't we all need love and appreciation?
- ☛ **Try being gallant.** It might be as simple as helping her take off her jacket in a restaurant, while you are dressed to kill and smelling great. Being a gentleman is back! A night of pampering at home can be gallant. Clean her house or apartment and serve a candlelight meal (pasta is easy), and flip on a CD of an Italian crooner like Andrea Bocelli.

For meals I suggest a few delicious recipes:

FOUR DELICIOUS, EASY-TO-COOK MEALS

1. Greek Salad

Ingredients: Diced feta cheese, 1 small onion cut in thin slices, 1 cucumber cut in medium slices, 1 tomato, cut in small wedges.

Directions: Put ingredients in a nice bowl. Pour in olive oil and vinegar, season to taste and mix. That's it!

2. Italian Pasta Sauce—light, easy and classy

Ingredients: **4** medium cloves of garlic, ½ cup olive oil, 1 large can or two small cans of diced tomatoes, 6 sliced mushrooms, 1 tablespoon Italian seasonings (also called herbs de Provence), pasta of your choice.

Directions: In saucepan, chop and sauté the garlic in the olive oil. Add the tomatoes and mushrooms. Stir in the Italian seasonings. Cook over medium heat for 30 minutes. Boil the pasta until al dente, and serve. How simple is that for a masterpiece!

Options: Meat-eaters can fry and add in a half-pound of chopped lean beef. The sauce is equally terrific with crabmeat or fish. Veggie-eaters can add chopped broccoli or vegetables of your choice and simmer for 10 minutes.

3. Exotic Egyptian Kushari

Ingredients: 1 cup lentils, 2 diced tomatoes, ¾ pound of fried chopped lean beef, light Italian pasta sauce as described above, 1 medium chopped onion, 1 cup rice, 1 cup elbow macaroni or the macaroni of your choice.

Directions: Boil the lentils in water until soft. Meanwhile, add the diced tomatoes and fried beef to the pasta sauce and cook for 20 minutes, stirring occasionally. Sauté the chopped onions until golden brown and set aside. When lentils have been cooking for 45 minutes, boil the rice and noodles for 10 to 15 minutes until tender. Mix the noodles, rice and sauce together and serve with browned onions on top. You're cooking for maybe an hour, and you're international!

4. Dessert Cherries Jubilee

Ingredients: A jar of unsweetened cherries and their juice, 1 tablespoon powdered sugar, 2 tablespoons flour, brandy or vodka

Directions: Put 5 tablespoon of the cherry juice (or water) in a cup and slowly stir in the flour until it forms a paste without lumps. In a shallow saucepan or frying pan, cook the cherries in the remaining juice on medium heat and immediately add the powdered sugar. Slowly mix the paste into the cherries and stir constantly for 5 minutes. Turn up the heat to medium high and bring to a boil. Pour about a third of a cup of the brandy or vodka over the top of the cherries and cook for another minute. If you are daring and have a gas stove, light the alcohol on the side of the pan for a romantic flaming effect. Pour over vanilla Häagen Dazs ice cream and serve. (Note: Practice this at least once before you present it.)

- **Be adventurous.** Make love in nature or against a wall, slow or wild. How about a picnic? A fun night of laughing and dancing? An evening drive in the moonlight? Wine and cheese? Holding her during sunset on a beach or at an intimate small-town hideaway, on top of a mountain or up on the roof?
- **Be imaginative.** Create an intimate ritual. Try writing down qualities you both want in your life, and those you want to let go. Then burn the letter.
- **Create fantasy and mystery.** Pretend you are strangers meeting at a designated place, kissing in a dark, narrow street. Enact a sexual fantasy with your woman as the main character. Bring out the "bad" that resides within most women. After all, how often does a good woman get the opportunity to be bad?
- **Be glamorous.** Watch a late-night movie and share drinks and food in bed, with her dressed in the glamorous nightgown you bought and you in the sexy underwear she bought. Or give her a day and night at a spa–alone or with you.
- **Be exotic.** On a Greek island, at a lone cafe bar on a pier jutting into the sea, candles barely flickering, the clink of crystal glasses merging with the light-hearted sounds of Vivaldi's Four Seasons wafting through the heavens, fishing boats inching across a dark crimson seascape into a panorama of misty isles. Get the picture?
- **Be elaborate.** Be her servant for the night! Shop for food and drink or cook an elaborate meal. Tack a menu outside the door. When she walks in, hand her a glass of champagne. Seat her and place her feet in a basin of soothing water as prep to a foot massage. After the massage, offer a taste of sherbet. She's your queen and you are her slave. Being elaborate might serve as a good Valentine's Day gift.
- **Traveling is always romantic.**

Plan ahead. Prepare a list of romantic ideas to pick from regularly, say, once a month. Start with her ideas of what is romantic. Write these ideas on the "Romance" Cheat Sheet (in the Appendix). Print the Cheat Sheet and place it in your wallet. If she likes spontaneous, and you are not, then plan spontaneous– a weekend visit to a charming nearby town, or someplace farther away. Want a remote location? Work out the logistics beforehand with the powers that be, to make room in her calendar.

Initiate action. Don't wait for a woman to initiate romance. She may desire romance, but you can bet your car she'll want her hero to initiate it.

Set the mood. Make it fun. Text her, promising some mysterious surprise at your place. (Hint: Sexy or humorous goes over well. Borrow material if you have to.) Arrive home early to scatter flower petals from the front door to the bedroom. She sees the vapor of a hot bath and candlelight. (Be careful! Heat causes drowsiness.) She smells strawberries, hears the pop of a champagne cork and the mood music you've put on the CD. Maybe a nice soft massage follows the bath. The conversation is humorous and intelligent. Want to get her hot and bothered? Make her feel sexy? If you are already intimate, undress her blatantly with your eyes. Then honestly, even humbly, flatter her flesh. Kiss her ever so slowly all over, especially over her eyes. She's yours.

Something in you attracted her. Discover what it is. (Hint: ask her!) Use this "something" to set the mood. A friend once said, "There is one particular quality we adore in the person we fall in love with." Remember what that quality is, and celebrate it. **Intimacy is romantic.** My friend Patricia says, "Friendship and romantic love cannot be achieved without intimacy, and intimacy depends upon the selective and voluntary disclosure of personal information that we don't share with everyone else." In other words, spend an intimate evening baring your soul and exploring her mind. Show that you want to know her highs and her frustrations (with minimal comment from you).

Caution. Even if she talks about her previous sexual exploits, be brief in telling yours.

<u>**Practice.**</u> Romance is an art form, and, as with painters, writers and basketball players, any art requires copious practice of its fundamentals and technique. Here are a few ideas to practice, practice, practice!

- Compliment her intelligence–always a winner, as it should be.
- Tell her you're wearing no underwear–in public.
- Ask her to raise her blouse in a car or train.
- Do something out of character, maybe a spontaneous hug.
- Dance to slow music, watching her dreamily.
- Be in tune with her mood and engage in sleazy love with a wicked smile.
- Stay at a Bed and Breakfast and serenade her.
- Kiss her when you go to bed and when you wake up.
- Tell her you love her–and mean it!

Caution. There is a distinction between romance and sex. Many men mistakenly think that any romantic moves on their part should inevitably lead to sex (like, in the next half hour). The danger, of course, is that the woman ends up not trusting your motives. Romancing is an ongoing process, like fertilizing your garden.

Practice being romantic.
Insert romantic ideas in the "Romance" Cheat Sheet
in the Attachments at the end of this book.

Communication Skills for the "Impaired"

In his book *The Five Love Languages,* Gary Chapman says that people use different languages to communicate different needs, and each of us is usually more fluent in one of those languages than the others. Chapman names these languages: touch, gifts, chores, words, and feelings. He says the problem is that while one person may communicate love through words, the other person can only understand love through words or touch or gifts. Communication has more moving parts than a wheat field in a storm. For example, we all grew up in our own family systems, and differences in the way we were raised may clash. In the house where I grew up, conflict was a way of life, but my wife's family avoids conflict the way we all avoid mosquitoes.

You can't possibly remember all the stuff you need to know about communication, but almost anyone can remember these three communication concepts:
- Listen to her for understanding.
- Ask questions to try and understand her.
- Talk about what you've heard her say.

Listen. Abraham Maslow, in his book The Psychology of Science, said, "To be able to listen–really, wholly, passively, self-effacingly listen–without presupposing, classifying, improving, controverting, evaluating, approving or disproving, without dueling with what is being said, without rehearsing the rebuttal in advance, without free-associating to portions of what is being said so that succeeding portions are not heard at all–such listening is rare."

Listening is not giving advice. How many times have you heard, "Stop telling me what to do! Just listen!"

Story: During a trying time in her life, the daughter of a good friend once courageously made this statement in an open letter to those close to her: "When you listen and accept that I feel what I feel, no matter how irrational, then I can quit trying to convince you and begin to understand what's behind this irrational feeling. When that's clear, the answers are obvious and I don't need advice."

Listening is not giving advice. Learn to say, "I might not be able to offer you solutions, but I can listen."

Ask questions that encourage her to talk about herself or clarify what has been said. This has two benefits: you get to know her better and you raise the conversation to a more intimate level. Questions are powerful. Asking them is a skill enhanced, as are most things, by practice. Most listening should be accompanied by questions, so **practice asking questions.**

The Roman Emperor Justinian said, "Everyone is his own universe." People are dying to talk about themselves, and there is something interesting about everyone. When we ask questions, we open up another's world and walk straight in. Try getting out of your universe and into hers.

We men often talk either too much or too little. Both can cause a one-way conversation.

Story: *As I was pulling a three-wood from my bag on the golf course, my occasional golfing buddy, a retired sixty-year-old woman, told me that what would make her most happy would be her husband talking to her about his activities. "He comes home after a busy day and, without saying much, turns on the TV," she said. "Then we eat dinner, watching TV in silence."*

You may feel that TV takes your mind off a busy day or reduces the boredom of the day-to-day, but regularly turn the TV off and talk to her.

Communication pitfalls to avoid: Dominating the conversation, being a know-it-all, getting into arguments and honestly expressing your feelings when there is a good chance the result will be disastrous. The first two are obvious, so we are going to focus on the last two.

Arguments. Benjamin Franklin said, "If you argue and rankle and contradict, you may achieve a victory sometimes; but it will be an empty victory because you will never get your opponent's goodwill.

Can you make someone happy when you argue with her?

My former business partner, a highly articulate man, goes silent during an argument. He once said something to the effect that, "Arguments are a waste of time; people aren't really listening to each other." So he doesn't engage.

If you want to please her, be her advocate. Look for areas of agreement to enhance the discussion.

Story: *I remember a conversation with the girlfriend of an acquaintance. She was so sure of everything she said! In the middle of what could have become a heated argument about in-vitro fertilization, I followed my own advice to look for areas of agreement, and forced myself to ask questions to fully understand her point. The argument quickly changed into a discussion, and before long we were each other's advocate.*

Because persistent arguments can kill relationships, I discuss them in greater detail in the section of this book called "Special Issues."

Honestly express your feelings. "Truth is beauty, beauty is truth," my grandmother used to say, quoting Keats. The most intimate times I have ever had were when I have been totally honest with someone. I let myself be vulnerable. That said, honestly expressing our feelings can often be, unfortunately, a trap. Finding the beauty in truth requires a listener who is open to hearing without judgment–someone who won't use the information as a battering ram against you in the future. **It takes self-esteem to listen without judging.** But you can't blame women for wanting honesty. What woman hasn't been lied to by a man who wants to get into her pants? The thing to remember is that everyone has a right to privacy and secrets, and truth that hurts should be revealed judiciously, and only if it serves the greater good.

Don't forget these communication suggestions:
- Avoid comparing her to another woman–or to anyone else for that matter–unless the comparison is favorable.
- Don't counsel a woman who hasn't asked for your advice.
- Be aware of these success words: we, our, us.
- **Tape Maslow's words on listening to a spot you will see again and again.**
- Balance listening, questioning, and talking.

Change One Thing for Her

The old saying goes, "A woman marries a man to change him..." So change one thing for her, even if it's to become her fix-it man and change the light bulbs around the house. My cousin has a *horny-do list*. "Nothing makes me hornier than my man fixing something," she once said.

In the movie *The Breakup,* with Jennifer Aniston and Vince Vaughn, Aniston says, "I want you to want to do the dishes once in a while." He replies, "Why would I want to do the dishes?" The relationship went downhill from there.

What's the big deal? Do the dishes for her once in a while! My wife wants me to look attractive in the morning, and I like being how I am, which means messy hair, droopy eyes, and, unfortunately, bad breath (not that I like bad breath). Of course it makes her happy when my hair is combed, teeth are brushed and eyes are washed before breakfast. So I do it. It takes five minutes, and the payback is that she has one less reason to be unhappy with me.

The one thing to change might be something she constantly complains about (which would have the added benefit of giving a respite from the complaining). I once saw a Klondike commercial in which a portly middle-aged guy walks into the kitchen and, while his wife watches, sets his glass on the counter. He then smiles at the camera and, to his wife's astonishment, picks up the glass and puts it in the dishwasher.

Message: It's important to her that you give a shit.

Change some aspect of yourself, just for her. (This applies whether she's your partner, lover, friend, mother, sibling, grandmother or daughter).

 **Tips**:

☞ Call her when you are going to be late. Show that you care. This will save you some grief!

☞ Say, "Screw the ballgame! What do you want to see on TV?"

☞ Review your wedding vows to make sure you're doing what you promised.

☞ Change your tone to one that is pleasing and appreciative, a tone free from cynicism or mocking.

☞ Kiss her tenderly behind the ear–just because.

☞ Feel the belly of your pregnant daughter, and confide how thrilled you are about becoming a grandpa.

You have to really want to change. Dale Carnegie said: "... put energy into who you want to be, and every thought will gradually turn you into that person."

Traditions: Keeping Romance Alive
By Rich Rawley

"... Creating your own traditions, and then keeping them over the years, brings a constant and deep sense of intimacy and togetherness that cannot be rivaled by any spontaneous acts of romance. The types of traditions you create are up to you. Most important is that they are your own." –W. Somerset Maugham

The truth is that love–like a plant, an animal or a human–has its own life. Any love has its infancy, childhood, teenage years, adulthood and old age. Many people view the latter stages as being boring and monotonous. But, just as some people enjoy the most active and exciting time of their lives in retirement, so love can continue to bloom with time. It doesn't happen by itself, of course. What would happen to a rose bush if it didn't have the benefits of love and tending, pruning and, certainly, weeding? Most of all, love needs some good fertilizer at the right time (organic, of course). Traditions are a natural source of romantic nutrients. A cherished tradition is one of the fertilizers of a relationship.

Value of traditions. Most long-lasting families have traditions of their own, which bind the members together and provide a solid foundation upon which they can cement their future. Families are not really different from any club or society: if you look closely, you will find they are all based on traditions that require effort and care. Neglect, whether in a couple, a family, among friends or in society, leads to stagnation and death.

One way to keep a relationship thriving is to establish your own private traditions.

Private, or personal, versus public. When we talk about personal traditions, we are not discussing big occasions like Christmas. Christmas is a public occasion, initially created by traditions set by someone other than you. Here we are talking about traditions that you as a couple develop around your own occasions, perhaps a tradition for your anniversary ("We always go to this restaurant," or "He always makes me a bubble bath, with candles and music"). It's not that Christmas and other major holidays are not important; it's just that they are unlikely to involve just the two of you.

For a newly formed couple, working out what to do for a big holiday can be traumatic. Let's imagine that Christmas is coming. How and where will you spend it? Alone? With her family? With your family? The more you discuss it, the more it seems like a no-win situation. While major public holidays are important, and they will contain special moments and feelings between the two of you, these days are shared with others. That's what makes your private traditions so special: you get to keep them all to yourself.

 **Tip:** To initially solve the "her family versus his family" dilemma, have one year with hers, one year with his, and one year on your own, just the two of you.

One way to start a tradition: borrow ideas. Sometimes you hear about someone's romantic or fun idea. Go ahead and borrow it! There are no copyrights on romantic traditions. Long ago, someone had the idea for the first romantic candlelight dinner. Now it's a classic. Borrow interesting ideas and adapt them to suit the two of you. In fact, go and seek out attractive new ideas you might be able to use. Check out the "Romance" section of this book. How about a picnic every May 1, or a night of dancing, or holding hands during sunset at an intimate small-town hideaway?

Start a tradition. Sure, it's easy to talk, but how do you actually start a tradition? It's not that hard! For example, "We always get a pizza on Friday nights!" Notice the enthusiasm. Or, along the same lines, develop a habit of going out for a nice dinner at Luigi's Restaurant after payday. After a while, the habit becomes a tradition. It may well happen without you being consciously aware of it, until after a few months or years you realize you almost always go out to Luigi's after payday. You've created a comfortable, easy tradition. There's no need for special preparation. It happens all by itself!

Begin your own sweet secret traditions. Let loose! It's just the two of you. Be silly if you want, serious if you like, or crazily romantic. It's your tradition. Some traditions are snuggly: on Wednesday nights we take the phone off the hook and watch a good movie. When was the last time you watched your favorite movie of all time? Make it a tradition. Go ahead, buy a copy. Maybe on Saturday mornings you can have breakfast in bed; or lounge around in bed all day watching animal shows while eating your favorite foods. Or you could start a charitable tradition. Maybe once a month you visit an animal shelter and help feed the dogs. Are you musical? Create a tradition of a night out at a concert.

For a weightier occasion, such as your anniversary, you may want to create several traditions–perhaps a special weekend away every second year, with fancy nights out when there is a full moon (Google the timings of the full moon). My favorite is the gifts-per-year tradition: for a five-year anniversary, five gifts, for ten years, ten gifts (but within the same budget). During our engagement, my wife and I decided that on each anniversary we would go out to dinner, perhaps at Luigi's, where we would take off our rings and lay them on the table. Then we would discuss whether we should put the rings back on. It's been many years for us, and the reasons to put them back on are still overwhelming.

For majorly important traditions, it will usually be necessary for you to capture the moment when the tradition is first happening–its birth. You might log it into your "soul-mate memory," for example, by saying something like, "This has been a great, great night. Let's do this every Valentine's Day for life!"

Of course, as time goes by you will both need to discuss whether your tradition deserves to continue to live, or whether the time has come for it to die a glorious death. In the space of a year, that great restaurant Luigi's may burn down, or you may find a place even better. Who knows? Be flexible, and let the new tradition be flexible as well.

How to keep traditions alive If left alone, traditions, like old generals, will fade away. Cultivate them! It's easy. There are five basic steps to keeping traditions alive.

1. Say what the tradition is (pretty simple, right?) and discuss it ahead of time–unless, of course, it is a surprise. Let the excitement build. Then write the tradition down in your "Keep Her

Happy" Cheat Sheet at the end of this book. Make plans around it. Give it life!

2. Don't be too rigid. A tradition is not ruined if it's celebrated a day early or late because something important has intervened. It's not the date on the calendar that is king; it's the meaning and reverence with which the event is celebrated. In this fast-paced era, rigidity will often bury tradition.

3. Toast the tradition when it arrives. Make a little speech. Tell her how happy you are to be with her again for this special occasion.

4. Reminisce about past celebrations as if they were happening today. Try and remember all the restaurants where you celebrated this tradition. What did she give you last year? Two years ago? Reminiscing about past good times allows them to live again. Don't pass up the opportunity.

5. Look to the future. Dream about what you will be doing next year on this same day, or two years from now, or five. Share your dreams, no matter how farfetched. "Next year, for our tenth, I want to take you to Venice." Even if it doesn't happen, dreaming about it together can bring you closer.

Following these five steps will give your tradition value and make its importance grow. It will invoke fond memories, emphasize good feelings, beliefs and passions, and give you both a happy glow as you look forward together into your mutual future. This is the power of good traditions: they unite.

 **Tips**:

- Good traditions are like sweet secrets: a private and personal link between you and your partner. The rest of the world knows nothing, except that something affectionate is going on with the couple exchanging knowing glances.
- Don't be a slave to your traditions. They should serve you, not the other way around.
- Keep the tradition fun. If it becomes a burden, you are trying too hard.
- Weed out traditions that have lost meaning. Merely going through the motions adds nothing to your life.
- Work at your traditions to keep them alive and vital. Make them special. Reminisce about past occasions and dream about the future.

Summary of the Basics

She deserves happiness!

- *Appreciate your mother, sister, cousin, aunt, friend, lover or the woman at the grocery store.*

- *Practice random acts of affection.*

- *Compliment a woman's intelligence, her looks, her dress, her scent...*

- *Practice being romantic. Add ideas to your "Keep Her Happy" Cheat Sheet. (p. 85)*

- *Balance listening, questioning, and talking.*

- *Change one thing for her.*

- *Establish traditions. They provide a solid foundation from which to build intimacy.*

GIFT-GIVING AND GIFT IDEAS

By Rich Rawley

Author Nan Robertson said, "Ever since Eve gave Adam the apple there has been a misunderstanding between the sexes about gifts." Well, let's finally get this one cleared up. Gift-giving is an art. Once you look at it from that perspective, it becomes a creative activity. It becomes fun.

"What? Shopping–fun?"

No, I didn't say shopping was fun. I am talking about gift-giving. Gifts are special when they come from the heart–something that in our modern, shopping-crazed world can be easily overlooked. But whether the gift is something you made yourself or bought, most important is the thought and effort that went into the selection.

Story: *The Pot. My family has a famous cooking pot. To this day, mere mention of it brings on laughs, grins, groans and a wave of storytelling. The pot has become a legend and is now considered to be somewhat of an heirloom. But that same pot very nearly ended up in the trash.*

On one of my parents' anniversaries, my father presented my mother with a special gift: this very pot. What kind of pot, you may ask? It was (and still is) a smallish, run-of-the-mill stainless steel pot with a practical handle and tight-fitting lid, the kind of pot you might use to heat up sauce or poach an egg. The kind of pot you might buy for yourself without much thought, because it's the one particular size you always seem to be missing. The kind of pot you don't think twice about after its purchase. It is, quite simply, an ordinary pot. And therein lies the problem.

A wedding anniversary (or partnership anniversary) is a very special event. For many happy couples, their anniversary is a day to remember and reaffirm their amazing, deeply personal vows of love and bonding. It is a rather private day, a day to be together and celebrate each other. It is a romantic day, a day to reflect on tender moments of the past, discuss the future, celebrate achievements, share a tear over losses and disappointments, and, at the end of the day, to honor that one person who is there for you more than anyone else in the world. For true romantics, it may well be the most important date on the calendar.

In choosing this pot as an anniversary gift, my father made a serious error in judgment. My mother, a wonderful cook, may have needed the pot. She may even have commented a few times that she didn't have quite the right pot for making sauce. She may have hoped that he might come home one ordinary day and casually say, "Oh, by the way, honey, I got you the type of pot you've mentioned a few times." But she certainly never imagined that he would buy this pot for their anniversary.

For those of you who are absolute beginners in the art of gift-buying, let me explain the problem. If your woman loves to cook and would absolutely fancy a super-quality pot extraordinaire with a gold or silver handle, then go for it, and get her some flowers to go with it. But no, an ordinary pot is not romantic. It speaks of heating spaghetti sauce and boiling eggs and scrubbing burnt-in gunk off the bottom.

My father's choice of an anniversary gift was terribly ill-advised. But at least he did one thing that seems to be beyond the grasp of all too many of us men—one thing that, in the end, made up for the choice. He remembered.

To this day, the mere mention of the pot causes instant laughter. It is a family heirloom, through which we remember their anniversary. What Mom knew, and what she knew some of her friends lacked, was that after years of trials and tribulations, her man loved her enough to remember their day.

***Remember special occasions and be a good gift-giver.
Sounds easy, doesn't it?***

Gift-Giving Occasions

- The big three: your anniversary, her birthday, Valentine's Day
- Mother's Day
- The no-special-occasion-whatsoever occasion
- Tough-guy gifts

The Big 3

Before we discuss the dos and don'ts of gift buying, we must first deal with these special occasions. On a basic level, as a lover and partner and a man who wants to please his woman, you are responsible for only three special occasions.

- Your anniversary. (Forgetting this date could land you in more trouble than forgetting her birthday.)
- Her birthday.
- Valentine's Day. (This is fairly easy to remember, since you cannot possibly fail to notice its rampant commercialism.)

Younger couples often have a tendency to remember too many occasions–the day we first met, our first date, our first kiss, etc. In a world of total romance, these would all be cherished days to be celebrated every year. Most of us probably have known a couple who, in the beginning, celebrated their month-ly anniversary too. Well, men, the good news is that once you are in a permanent relationship and you have a specific anniversary, you no longer have to deal with monthlies.

Three special days! How simple is that? Apparently, it's not so easy. The poor sod who has forgotten his anniversary yet again has been the center of so many sitcoms and farcical plots that you might think it could never actually happen. But it is precisely because it happens so often that it remains a comedy favorite (although calling it a tragedy might be more appropriate).

Story: Forgetting the Big One. *My good friend Eric was looking decidedly down when I visited him at work. "Close the door," he said when I popped into his office. "I want to tell you something." Eric is a big, rugby-playing teddy bear of a man who looks like he could crush you in one of his massive arms. But he is playful, fun and sensitive. And he is, concerning his anniversary at least, a far-too-typical man. He failed to do what my dad had remembered. No gift. Not even a pot.*

Eric was blue. The day before, his wife had phoned him several times. He has an important job, and although his wife phones him at the office from time to time, it is uncommon for him to receive several calls in one day from her. That night when he went home, she was acting strange–expectant, you might say. Then, when she realized that he wasn't just pretending–that he really didn't have flowers secretly hidden in the car or reservations at their favorite restaurant or a gift in his jacket pocket–the game was up.

When a man bemoans his fate to a male friend, he is hoping to get an expression of sympathy. "Yeah, I know how you feel. I forgot our anniversary two months ago. I'm still in the doghouse." But, as you might expect, I was not going to give Eric such reassurances. I wanted to know how he could forget his anniversary in the first place.

"Oh, that was easy," he said. "It wasn't actually my fault." He had dutifully entered the anniversary in his iPhone ages ago, but he had been in meetings all that day and had not turned his iPhone on. So, in fact, it was the iPhone's fault! And yes, he had tried to use this lame excuse on his wife. Needless to say, it did not cut much wood.

What would I advise someone in Eric's situation? First of all, I would tell him to admit to his wife how badly he felt, declare himself decisively in the doghouse, and then bring flowers home, again and again and again for the rest of the week. And it goes without saying that a surprise romantic dinner at her favorite restaurant would be in order. Now, there are recent surveys that say women don't prefer flowers. Ignore them. It's still the thought that counts–plus the night out.

Don't Get Caught in the Anniversary Trap. Make your anniversary a "couple event." It is your mutual anniversary, not just hers. Many couples have an arrangement in which nothing is said about the anniversary until the day itself. Then, when (or if) the man presents her with flowers or chocolates, the woman says something like, "Oh honey, you remembered!" This is a trap! It is a surefire way of guaranteeing that one day you will forget. Eric and his wife could have been discussing the anniversary at least a week or so ahead of time, making plans, fishing for gift ideas, building anticipation and adding to the suspense and excitement. Like putting Christmas decorations on the tree, the advance preparation adds up to making the big day even more special.

Make your anniversary a special tradition. Discuss it in advance. Get excited! If you are talking about it a week in advance, you won't forget the day. But just in case, how about circling the date on your calendar with a big red heart? When she sees the heart, you might get a bonus. Do whatever it takes to make you remember!

As a memory aid, we have included space in the "Keep Her Happy" Cheat Sheet (page 85) for your anniversary and her birthday. Fill it in right now!

No Surprises–Her Birthday. Her birthday is a little less special than the anniversary because it is a public day. Anyone who knows her may remember and celebrate her birthday. But that doesn't mean you shouldn't make it special. I try to keep her birthday simple–a good meal at her favorite restaurant, with us all dressed up. But right now I am going to read through the "Romance" section of our book for some good ideas. Why don't you join me?

Remembering the birthdays of special people in your life can be very meaningful to them. It doesn't take much effort. I have a friend who has a terrific memory for special dates and phone numbers. We don't see each other often, but every year on my birthday he calls to sing me "Happy Birthday." It makes me feel special and has kept our friendship alive when the time and distance between us could have ended it. I don't have his memory, but, inspired by his thoughtfulness, I have made a list of the birthdays of all the people who are important to me. I keep it in a see-through plastic cover on my desk. When a birthday on the list comes up, I give a call or send a short e-mail or text message. That's all it takes.

Valentine's Day. Many people scoff at Valentine's Day. They claim it was seized upon by greedy marketers and is nothing more than the creation of greeting-card companies. Yes, yes, I know. But it's still a good idea. Nothing says you have to fall for the commercial hype. Celebrate it for what it really should be: a day for lovers, a day for the two of you. Create your own personal Valentine's Day traditions.

The fact that you remember your anniversary, her birthday and Valentine's Day will always remain the most important aspect of these special occasions. It was remembering my parents' anniversary that saved my father. His intention was sincere, and my mother reports that the pot has proven to be reliable and trusty. It now has a chip on its handle and a few scratches here and there, but the pot is a much cherished keepsake. The man who gave it is no longer with us, yet his good intentions and the deep love between my parents remain with my mother, symbolized, quite ironically, by that simple pot.

- ***Plan your anniversary together and mark it on your calendar, circled in a heart.***
- ***Fill out the "Keep Her Happy" Cheat Sheet.***
- ***Remembering the event itself is the most important aspect of a special occasion.***

Now that we have covered the big three, we can move on to other gift-giving days and the art of gift-giving.

Mother's Day

How can you forget your mother? Most mothers love unconditionally, which is to say that they are there for us in dark and gloomy days, as well as when everything is lollipops and rainbows and our team's on top. My mom loves me unconditionally, and her house is another home for me if ever I need one. On Mother's Day, show her you care. If you can't think of a gift, pick a few from this book. Update the "Keep Her Happy" Cheat Sheet.

Many years ago, I arranged to deliver two lobsters to my grandmother in Long Island each Mother's Day. They were delivered by a mysterious-looking messenger and accompanied by a card that simply said, "An ardent admirer." My grandmother loved the lobster and the mystery of it all. She kept trying to figure out who the admirer was, although I believe she knew. I enjoyed the suspense as much as she did.

Don't ever forget Mother's Day!

No-Special-Occasion-Whatsoever Occasion

I am about to make a controversial statement, which many of you may find shocking: As a man who wants to make his woman happy, you will be responsible for buying her gifts every once in a while for no reason whatsoever. Yup, that's right! It's not her birthday, not your anniversary, not Valentine's Day. It's just an ordinary, regular, run-of-the- mill Tuesday. Or Monday. Or Thursday. And yet you still buy her a gift. Why?

It's simple. You want to please her and you don't need a special occasion to do it. The very fact that the occasion is ordinary will make her even happier, and she will want to make you happy in return–perhaps with that smile that's only for you, an I-love-you kiss or something only she can think of.

No-reason-whatsoever is often the most rewarding kind of gift-giving. It's unexpected. Coming up with original and pleasing ideas presents a creative challenge, but you will find plenty of them below and in the "Romance" chapter. Women love this stuff, and it's easy and inexpensive, as we will demonstrate. So what's the problem? "It's not cool," you say. "Real men don't need to buy their women flowers or chocolates." After years of getting nothing, a woman may play into this dribble by claiming that random gifts are not important. Trust me, that is just an ego-protecting mechanism.

It's spring. The tulips are in bloom. You bring home a small bouquet for no reason. You might say, "These were so pretty I had to buy them for you," or "I saw these tulips and they brought back memories of our first spring together."

Frequency. The trick is to give something every once in a while. Sounds dead simple! Hint: giving a gift every day is too often, except perhaps when your love is new, and once every three months is too rare. We suggest once a month. But make it unpredictable. Don't buy flowers every Wednesday, or a bottle of wine every second Thursday. Variety is the spice of romance.

What to give. There is no end to the possibilities. Remember, it is not the price that counts but the thought. Let's start with the classics.

- **Flowers.** When it's not a special occasion, buy a few flowers, or just one. Three and five are great numbers. Choose an odd number (odd numbers look better in a vase). You don't need to wrap them. If you must wrap them, select plain paper, no ribbons or bows. Remember, you want to appear casual. If you are feeling romantic or especially in love, go for a single long-stemmed rose. One flower can say a lot. Otherwise, go with what looks good, like tulips or lilies. Ask for help in the shop if you need it.

- **Chocolates.** Go for something you know she likes or try something new. A chocolate bar, unless it's a really special kind, is not acceptable. For a fun evening of chocolate delight, start with milk chocolate, move on to bittersweet (containing over 50% cocoa), and finish up with chocolate that has a very high cocoa content (over 70%; Lindt has a bar that is 99% cocoa). Give her a sliver-sized piece of this last one and tell her to allow it to melt. No chewing! This is a sensual and romantic anytime gift idea. Don't overdo it, though. Many women have come to view chocolate-giving as a ploy to get them into bed. Don't use it for that–although if such ends up being the result, well, you can't refuse it.

- **Other ideas.** Her favorite bottle of wine, two tickets to see a show, a forty-minute massage; clean the bathroom (not sexy, but it shows love); arrange a baby-sitter for a night out; pack a picnic basket and pick her up for lunch. For more suggestions, see the "Keep Her Happy" Cheat Sheet (page 85).

How to give your no–special-occasion gift. Don't make a big deal about it. The first few times, you may be tempted to gloat (especially if the reaction you get is as positive as what usually happens). Restrain yourself! When she asks why you bought the gift, use the flower response above, or tell her you bought it because you love her. And you do, right? Even if she resorts to the classic line, "Okay, what did you do wrong?" stick to your guns with something from the heart. "When I thought of you, I had to buy flowers." Don't make a speech, just a line or two. After all, this is not a special occasion. It's just a Tuesday, or a Thursday, or a Monday.

Tough Guy Gifts

Are you a tough guy? A real man? If so, you are exactly the kind of man many women are looking for. And you have a natural advantage over softer guys: when you do something like surprise her with flowers or with a special meal you made yourself, it will make a stronger impression.

Wait a minute, you may be thinking, *tough guys don't buy flowers! They sure don't cook!*

Maybe you have a point. Tough guys certainly don't buy flowers for their own apartment or do gourmet cooking as a hobby. But a tough guy with flowers? For any woman, that's a sight that's hard to beat. Try this. Get your muscles all pumped up, put on a tight T-shirt that shows them off, then buy a bouquet of flowers and walk down the street. Heads will turn–both men's and women's. They are not thinking, look at that pussy! Nope, they're thinking, *now there goes a real man! I wonder who the lucky lady is.*

Maintain your personal style and try to see the powerful contrast between your usual tough-guy image and the same guy with a bouquet of flowers. It's the stuff of romance novels, which means it gives you a real edge. Your partner knows you are tough. Giving her flowers won't make her think you've gone soft. The gift will just make you even more irresistible to her.

"Keep Her Happy" Cheat Sheet

We are only men, after all, famous for forgetting events like anniversaries and birthdays. Keeping your woman happy can require a fair bit of memory work. To make remembering a bit easier for you, we are including a special cheat sheet in the attachments at the end of this book. The cheat sheet includes:

IMPORTANT DATES like her birthday, your anniversary, etc.
SHOPPING - waist, blouse or bra sizes, for example.
SIMPLE ANYTIME GIFTS
FLOWER RULES

If there is something you don't know, find out in a subtle way. If you are a typical man, this sheet will be a lifesaver!

I keep a cheat sheet in my wallet because I desperately need it when buying her clothes. We can remember our anniversaries, but bra size and variations in clothing size are usually unsolved mysteries. Now I don't need to describe my wife's bra size to the sales-lady by holding up my cupped right hand and saying, "They're, you know, this size."

Secret or not? Should you keep your cheat sheet a secret? Use your judgment. At first, my wife didn't know I had one. When I told her about it one day, I could see she was very pleased I had gone to the trouble.

Keep one in your desk or …? No system is foolproof. Remember my poor friend Eric, who stored his anniversary date in an smartphone. For a backup, keep a copy of your cheat sheet in a spot where you are sure to see it from time to time. Write a post-it note saying "Cheat Sheet" to trigger you into action.

Go to Attachments at the end of this book, cut out and fill in the *"Keep Her Happy"* Cheat Sheet **now!**

Gift-Giving Summary

- *Remember special occasions.*

- *Celebrate the Big Three special occasions. And don't forget Mom!*

- *Plan your anniversary together. Mark it on your calendar circled in a heart.*

- *Give her a no-special-occasion gift; turn an ordinary day into something to remember.*

- *Fill out the "Keep Her Happy" Cheat Sheet in the Attachment on page 85.*

SPECIAL ISSUES

We grew up in a disposable world. Throwaway cans, coffee cups, plates–even cars. Shoemakers have disappeared; it's cheaper to buy a new pair. Fashion changes and clothes are ditched after a season. TVs, stereos and gaming machines are replaced as soon as a new technology comes along. It's only natural that people have begun to think that relationships are as disposable as running shoes and stereos (although I know more than a few men who would never dream of disposing of their high-end stereo equipment). But disposable relationships carry hidden costs: bitterness, resignation, cynicism, callousness and the despair of waking up in an empty bed.

It is precisely because we live in a disposable world that people everywhere are rediscovering that quality adds value. With regard to things, good workmanship and excellence of materials are worth preserving and maintaining. Relationships, too, need workmanship.

So the next time you toss a disposable coffee cup, think about how much better the coffee would have tasted in porcelain. Likewise, if you've been through a disposable relationship, you must know that there is great promise in making efforts to preserve an existing relationship. You owe it to yourself to make the effort to enhance your relationship and experience the difference in quality. Having and keeping anything worthwhile takes effort, whether it's your jump shot, your job or your relationship.

We all have issues that cause our relationships with women to go stale or break down, but keep in mind that if you let your love down, it will die.

Removing Roadblocks to Her Happiness

There are a few roadblocks that men have struggled with since we left the Garden of Eden:

- We want to make her happy, but our egos get in the way.
- We get caught in the victim/bad guy scenario.
- We let our communication routinely take the form of criticism and arguments.
- We don't know how to cope with crying.

We want to make her happy, but our egos get in the way. How many of us have screwed up with a woman because our ego got in the way? How many times have you let a situation or a discussion go bad because your ego got in the way of responding to her words properly, even though deep down you knew what she meant? You took her words to mean something that fit into your scenario, something that justified your anger or hurt. Then, of course, you responded within this contrived scenario in just the way that would later fill you with remorse and regret.

Aren't most of our issues with women about ego? Doesn't ego get in the way when we are jealous, or when we can't hear her because our pride has been wounded, or because we dominate the conversation in some way that gives our ego satisfaction, or because she's impossible at times and our egos cannot adjust? Ego can turn small disagreements into big arguments because the past accumulation of baggage does not let us focus on the issue at hand.

Facing a man's ego can be overwhelming. It's like facing a huge boulder precariously perched on a mountain, just waiting to topple downhill. Ego often kills intimacy and strikes a blow at a woman's self-esteem. The result is usually a miserable situation for us.

Do any of these sound familiar?

- She says no to sex. You become agitated and then incensed, or you fume inside. Rejection hurts! You toss off a few biting remarks, camouflaging your anger so she can't see your damaged pride.
- She criticizes some small action of yours and you blow up, spewing the volcanic ash of her past sins. The attack words hurt her, and the ash builds.
- She's talking and you cut her off, because what you have to say is more important.
- You misinterpret her, and thus the truth never gets the opportunity to set you free.

Consider what the outcome would be if, in a brief, fleeting moment of cognition during an argument, while hovering on the brink of fury, you asked yourself, will I end this relationship, or will I get back to loving her?

If you know that the happy times will come again, then why waste time being angry? Trust that one day you will get your point across, and she will hear you. Okay, so she's not listening to you now, but you've made your point before and you will be able to make it again. Imagine the refreshing change in routine if, instead of tossing useless innuendos and barbs, you became her advocate instead of just your own. What would she do? What a challenge! Now, I realize that being her advocate in a fight with you is as hard as throwing a touchdown in a blizzard. But it is possible. (Just to make you feel better, I can tell you that this happens to be the major challenge of my life.)

The reality is that if you want good relationships with women, it helps to occasionally be the humble person. You have the power.

Remove ego by using Dale Carnegie's suggestion: "Picture in your mind the person you want to be, and each thought is hourly transforming you into that person." Rummage through old photos of yourself to find that humble person within. If he's nowhere to be found, take a picture of yourself in a pose of imagined humility. Frame it, hang it somewhere visible and challenge yourself to throw the touchdown in the blizzard.

The victim/bad guy scenario. You know it well.
- She does something–whatever!
- Ego aroused, you get angry.
- She goes silent.
- You try to reason, over and over, using logic to explain yourself.
- Using few words, she disagrees, conveying that she is hurt–and it's your fault. Any attempt at defense is useless.
- Feeling the frustration of once again being the bad guy, you go on the offensive, thus proving her assertions.

The victim/bad guy scenario is a predictable event. Victims rarely see the other's point of view. Why should they? They have been wronged. So how do you get a win-win?

Walking away may seem to help, and often provides a cooling off period, but generally it prolongs our agony and guilt. No, I'm afraid there is no win other than to accept that humility is a desirable virtue to have when dealing with women. If you want a mellow life, learn to listen instead of explaining. If this approach offends your sense of manhood, keep in mind what Will Rogers said: "There are two theories about arguing with a woman. Neither one works."

Arguments and criticism. Ever been in this situation? To end a bitter argument, she briefly offers an olive branch (you've seen it–a giggle, a visible softening, a tear), but you just can't bring yourself back from the brink of rage to acknowledge her effort. You can't relax your breathing, find some humor, or honestly expose your sensitive feelings, because you're pissed. Instead, you pass over that fleeting moment of cognition, when you have choice, and continue the battle.

The situation gets out of control. The next thing you know, you're inserting past hurts into the argument. Maybe you storm out of the room or go for a beer. You sleep on the couch that night, and the next day you avoid each other.

In my book, *Breaking Free*, I talk about love being like a bank account. When you first start out, you make lots of deposits. Arguments and criticism are withdrawals. Do you have a positive balance? Criticism is probably at the heart of most arguments. Arguments and criticism hang out together.

When you think about it, criticism is about trust. Generally, the longer the relationship, the more you criticize. Remember, you come from different family systems, you are of different genders, and you have personalities that are usually the opposites of each other.

Of all of the issues associated with getting along, arguments and criticism are the hardest for me to overcome. They are relationship killers. Using some of the advice given in this book, I have done a lot better coping with arguments. For instance, here is a suggestion to avoid arguments:

Pick a time that's agreeable to both of you for talking.

With an egg timer, take turns talking for three minutes. Rule: no interrupting.

Use the egg timer three times each. Remember, no interruptions! You will generally find that after you've each had three turns, your issues are more clearly understood. If there is no resolution, shelve the discussion until the next day and try again.

Also, the *always rule* is: you can get more with honey than vinegar.

For me, minimizing criticism is more difficult. I generally have long-term relationships, and as relationships age trust can become more and more of an issue. Suddenly, what used to be good advice becomes, "All you do is criticize me." Once you get to that point, you are in deep doo-doo.

When criticism from either one of you becomes an overwhelming element in the relationship, maybe you need a therapist. But the reality might be that you have just become lazy; that you're angry about your partner's past transgressions; that the fervor of your love has waned along with your trust. This is my biggest challenge: I have been lazy. Rereading the techniques I've used in this book, I realize now that I've not been romantic in a while, have not complimented her like I used to. As of this moment, I am committed to spending more time romancing my wife. I am going to make more deposits in the love account.

Coping with crying. I promised my cousin Sharon that when she had her second child I would visit and help out. Over the span of two weeks with my nephews (one, three months old, and the other a two-year-old), I noticed ten reasons that babies cried: they were sitting in piss or shit, hunger, lack of attention, they hurt themselves, they did not get what they wanted, they became frustrated with their physical limitations, they did not want to go to bed, someone yelled at them, they didn't like what was being done to them or for them, or for no apparent reason.

Helping out with Sharon's children got me thinking about crying in general. You don't need a psychologist to make a few simple observations about people as they age:

- Boys are conditioned to stop crying, and thus later on are seen as emotionally stunted (but honestly, who really wants a guy who habitually cries?), even though they become unhappy for many of the same reasons they cried as babies.
- Girls are not conditioned to stop crying as much as boys are, and, as women, they seem to retain many of the reasons they cried as babies.

When I bring up with women the subject of crying, however, I have to be very careful to treat it with respect. Crying is a sacred cow (a way of coping, perhaps). Reasons women have given me for crying:

- "I'm angry."
- "I can't control my emotions, or I'm overwhelmed by them."
- "It's the only thing I can control."
- "Sometimes I cry because it seems like the only thing to do."
- "It's the appropriate response to a situation."
- "I'm in pain."
- "I know men can't stand it."

In general, men make distinctions between different types of crying. They seem to be astute at recognizing and understanding what I will call A-type cries, like when something horrible has happened, or our woman misses us terribly, or she has hurt herself, or even, occasionally, when she cries for no apparent reason. I've generally noticed that men treat these cries in a sensitive, caring and responsible manner.

Conversely, I think it can also be said that men generally can't understand what they intuitively interpret, or misinterpret, as what I will designate as B-type crying. B-type crying has been known to frustrate, blackmail, elicit guilt, and seriously impede communication. B-type crying would include "Things are not going my way", "Fuck you, I'm angry", "You hurt my feelings", and "I don't like what is being done to me, or for me." B-type crying most often creates a helpless or nervous reaction in men that causes us to bolt out of the room and out the door. Why do you suppose this is?

If you seek a way to cope with crying and please her, check out these suggestions:
- Listen, don't talk.
- Know the dates of her period. During grumpiness and tears say: "Would you like a cup of tea, my dear?"
- At times of anger, revenge, and general emotional discontent, a kind word turns wrath to "Thank you, baby."
- When she wakes up unhappy in the morning, start her off with "Good morning, sweetie," or your own endearing equivalent. Make this a habit.
- When she cries in the middle of an argument, think about humility and consequences. Say, "You are right on that point." Repeat her point, then suggest a timeout. During the break, imagine her happy.
- At menopause, listen! Be very careful with jokes. Commiserate. No advice, please!

- When you catch her nose doing a cry-wrinkle, or when moisture starts to fill her eye sockets, say softly and earnestly, "How are you doing, sweetie?" Then listen! Listen! Listen!

That's it! End of story.

Reactivating Long-Term Relationships

In the beginning, she was perfect. Your brand-new life exploded with the excitement and profound intimacy fundamental to a new couple. You had found your other half. She completed you. She trusted you and listened to your stories and advice. There was nothing you couldn't do together. Birds sang sweetly. Stars twinkled. You were falling in love, with no end in sight. Life with her was fun. You were playful.

Time passed. You got to know each other. The love deepened, matured. You learned more about her body and mind and habits, and when the falling-in-love neatly transformed itself into being-in-love, you could show your weakness with the assurance that trust and security brings to partners. Your gentle kiss behind the ear reminded her, and you, that you were soul-mates.

Somewhere along the journey, "in love" became a seldom-used expression. Yes, you still love her, but existence feels commonplace, even dull. You dream–like Lester Burnham, the father in the movie *American Beauty*–of fooling around with young, eye-catching hotties. She is always correcting what is never good enough. Sometimes you find yourself lying to avoid her scrutiny. And your sex life? Erosion has replaced explosion. She seems tired of your touch. You don't fulfill her needs, and she is clueless about yours. These days, communicating with her is like climbing a tree while wearing hiking boots, winter gloves, and a forty-pound pack–it's hard work just hanging on. Now the opposites that attracted you grate against each other. She resents your advice, perceives it as criticism. Lately, the gender jokes and funny lists of differences between men and women on the internet apply to you more and more. Trust is in decline.

But you love her, nonetheless. You like being with her. You respect her, you really do. But you're wondering what, exactly, love means, because the fun and playfulness have faded as sunset fades into night. Let's face it, you're in a rut.

Is the rut your fault? Hers? Or does the average modern couple cohabitate too closely, without enough breathing room? Are we men isolated once the mating chase is over? And do we thus lose the delight of intimacy?

I often ask women if their husbands or long-term boyfriends have friends they can talk to. They usually say, "Yes, he's got lots of friends." Pursuing the issue further, I ask, "Who does he talk to if he has a problem with your relationship?" Invariably, after a thoughtful pause, her tone changes, becomes concerned. "You know," the response goes, "I've been trying to get him to make an intimate friend he can talk to."

Why is this? Do we men tend towards being loners, relinquishing to women the responsibility to maintain social contact and thus isolating ourselves? For men, is isolation an eventual, inevitable state of being?

Story: *During my travels in Egypt, in the desert oasis of Aswan I met Randy, a wiry, freckle-faced man of twenty-five. Randy told me how his dad had isolated himself. "One of the reasons I travel is because I don't want to wind up like him," Randy said. "We live a comfortable life, but my dad is cynical and bored at fifty-one, and he likes to quibble with Mom. He works all the time, comes home late, and is too tired to do anything but flip on the TV and bitch at Mom and the Democrats for giving away his hard-earned money. I'm not going to spend my old age on a sofa worrying about my assets."*

It's not easy maintaining our equilibrium in this fast-paced culture. We are steeped in fantasy, sex you can watch, youth, and the what-have-you-done-for-me-lately level of loyalty. Work defines us, our "coupleness" defines us, our kids define us, and our responsibility defines us–to the extent that perhaps we have lost our identity, our oomph. But maybe if Randy's dad kept a little romance going with his wife and his life, he could avoid his own decline.

If any of the above fits you, what are you prepared to do? You can choose to change something, to reactivate the spark that made you fall in love–and, possibly, reactivate your existence. Here are some thoughts on the subject:

Acknowledge that you are responsible for letting your relationship deteriorate. Then, focus on the positive.

Story: *When my friends Jack and Debbie got married, Debbie said it was destiny. Time went by. Jack started to spend more hours at work than at home. He progressed quickly and became a manager at an accounting firm. They began to fight about work, money and appreciation. He said she was bankrupting him with her spending. She countered with all the things she did as a mother and wife, and with remarks about his weight and his love affair with work. He said that work was hard, that she never exercised, that she'd been eating a lot of chocolate lately. It went on and on.*

Debbie met another guy who honored her and treated her as someone special. After the initial intrigue, she eventually left Jack for greener pastures where the sun shone every day. Jack was devastated, depressed, and lonely. He missed her laughter and humor. He said she'd kept his life vital.

After the pheromones stopped flying around at warp speed, Debbie admitted that the new man had a dark side to him. Just about the time when Jack started dating other women, Debbie gave signals that she would accept him back.

Jack was no fool. He could easily have let his hurt ego rule the situation. But he didn't. He considered all the things they enjoyed together, how their philosophies fit. Jack realized that without Debbie's sparkle, his existence would only be about the job. He let go of his gripes and proclaimed to her, "As far as I'm concerned, we're partners for life."

Jack focused on the positive. He made Debbie feel special again. He began a ritual of kissing her every morning to start the day and every night to end it. He followed the advice of Andy, the farmer: "You treat a woman good—and she treats you great!"

Jack still works hard, but Debbie doesn't seem to mind as much now, because he pays more attention to her and considers her a true partner.

Admire her. One characteristic of all good relationships is that the two people genuinely admire each other. My two uncles had terrific marriages with my aunts, both strong-minded women. The uncles occasionally spoke words that indicated their admiration, but mostly you could see it in their eyes and in the smiles they aimed towards my aunts. The aunts invariably noticed, and electricity passed between them. Happy relationships are about trust, and admiration is a central ingredient.

Change one thing for her. It's hard to change, but change is the key to reactivating a long-term relationship. Remember the old saying, "A woman marries a man to change him." So change one significant thing for her.

Above all—and this is a true test of memory—go back to being the man you were when you fell in love.

Fixing What Is Broken

Fixing a relationship means improving your situation to the point where you are happy.

Story: *At one point during the writing of this book I sent e-mails to women I knew asking them what made them happy. I also asked them to forward my e-mail to women they knew. One day I received an e-mail from Dani, a friend of a friend. She said she was a housewife responding to my question. Actually, she began the e-mail in a state of depression about what was definitely broken without possibility of repair. Then she got around to the happy part.*

"What made me happy?" Dani wrote, before answering with sarcasm. "Taking my first Prozac at breakfast when I can still hope it will make my day. Sending my kids to school, knowing I won't see them for eight hours. Hearing the clock ring eleven times in the a.m. and thinking it's a decent time to fix myself a Martini–it's aperitif time, after all! Reading that money sent for victims of the tsunami was seized by corrupted local governments, and knowing I was smart not to send any. Having an out-of-town working alcoholic husband. Keeping arguments, sex and other boring marital duties to a minimum …"

You can safely say that Dani was not a happy woman. Her marriage and her life were kaput. When your relationship is broken, as hers was, you have three basic alternatives:

- Move on to greener pastures.
- Keep suffering with your current relationship.
- Commit to fix what has been broken.

Now comes the other half of Dani's letter, about moving on to greener pastures with a new man.

"My happiness as a woman," she continued, *"is strongly linked to a feeling of independence and freedom. I need to feel I'm being me, before being the wife, mother, employee, friend of … For a long time after my divorce, I thought sharing my life again with one person was unthinkable. I saw a relationship as a space where each partner has to give up something to make it liveable. Eventually I met my current husband and discovered what I call the lighthouse principle.*

"I used to be free, but freedom was dangerous; I could lose my way and myself. So I set up limits, and dear freedom became limited. But now I don't mind having less freedom, because I have somebody who waits for me and respects my choices, while wanting to share them or even while challenging them. This allows me to grow and experience. I can try anything, because if I get lost, have doubts, make mistakes, I can go back to the coastline and follow his light to safety. He's my lighthouse.

"He said I'm his lighthouse, too. I now live in a relationship where a big space is filled with attraction, admiration, willingness to discover, understanding, sharing and pleasing each other. It makes me happy. The sea gets rough sometimes and the sky cloudy, but I'm not afraid to lose what I've got. If my lighthouse goes, I know I will find a new one because I know what to look for."

Moving on is an agonizing decision, but sometimes, ultimately, you have to stop the pain and begin again, like Dani. The never-ending misery is when you just suffer with your current relationship, languishing between moving on and committing to change what you have, unable to make a decision or move in any direction.

Story: I once sat at a table in a Thai restaurant next to a couple dressed for business. They were fighting with the type of intensity that has no awareness of those around them. Each was focused on being right, being a victim, being understood, being appreciated, being defensive.

"If you would only listen to me just once!" he whined. "You don't seem to recognize the positive things I do."

"You've worn me down with these constant fights," she responded with an air of righteous desperation.

"Nothing is ever your fault, is it? It's always me. I wear you down! I do this, I do that! What about you? You're always picking, picking, picking!"

"Maybe that's what happens to people who are always right."

"What does that mean?"

"It means that I am so sick of your impenetrable ego!"

There was a short lull before he resumed, using a multitude of explanatory words. She evaded him with brevity, as if his words were arrows to be deflected by a shield. They went on and on, each saying just enough to tweak the other. Frustration poured from the very core of their wounded hearts, chilling the air between them as their pad Thai and mango salad lay on the table, aging and ignored.

It pained me to listen, and I could barely restrain myself from leaning their way and screaming, "Stop it! You're going nowhere. What you are saying doesn't matter. It doesn't matter, believe me! I've been there. Your words are falling on deaf ears!"

Suffering with your relationship is a choice. Committing to fixing the problem means getting rid of the past. The past chains you to a bad attitude. Sometimes it helps to take a break specifically designed to achieve a measure of independence from each other, in order to get the romance or friendship back. It's a risky business, but change requires risk and, often, an experience of freedom from the environment you live in.

My first wife and I had a ten-year honeymoon before storm clouds moved in. After another ten years of dealing with the on-and-off storm, we decided to separate for six months.

We'd known couples who'd separated for two to three months, and it never worked. Either they weren't away from each other long enough to remember what they'd once had or they were gone long enough to know that what they'd once had was completely lost. Separation was a risk, but as a youth I had mentally taken an oath never to fight the way my mother and father did. My wife hated the thought of separation, but she added a few months for good measure, lengthening the separation to a year. At the very least, separation would provide a respite from our droning arguments, like that of the couple in the Thai restaurant.

I had never lived alone. I'd always had family or college roommates, and I got married while in graduate school. But, living alone, I learned about quiet and the sense of independence and freedom Dani spoke of. I even learned about appreciating the many chores that devoured my wife's day. I found that most friends gave advice that reflected their situations, not mine. I also learned that my body showed the vulnerability that my mind refused to admit. For a week, I couldn't lift my head because of a serious neck problem that flared up from the tension of it all.

After a while, my wife and I began dating each other and I learned how to romance her again. For her part, she loved the renaissance. When the sabbatical ended, we wrote a partnership agreement, starting with what we liked about each other and stating our goals for living together happily.

By separating, we'd changed the landscape long enough to live happily with our differences for the next five years. And, although we finally divorced, the sabbatical helped us leave the relationship when it no longer fit, while maintaining friendship and respect for each other.

Fixing what you have takes commitment, courage and risk. As discussed earlier, relationships are like a garden: some last forever and some for only a short time. Plants need to be cared for. They need pruning, sunlight, water and earth that is occasionally aired and mixed with fertilizer. So, if your relationship is broken, decide whether you are willing to commit to working on the problem by ripping out the past, getting a little fresh air and starting the fertilizing process. Otherwise, make yourself and, maybe, some other woman happy by moving on. Either way, you take a big risk. But the biggest risk to happiness, both yours and hers, is doing nothing. Nothing ventured, nothing gained.

Special Issues Summary

- **Remove ego and listen.**

- **Focus on the positive, and remember:**

  ✓ *Admire her.*
  ✓ *Change one thing for her.*
  ✓ *Go back to being the man before
    the wedding.*
  ✓ *Commit to fix the problem, or move on.*
  ✓ *Tend the garden.*

BECOMING A MAN WHO MAKES WOMEN HAPPY

"I must be willing to give up what I am,
in order to become what I will be."
– Albert Einstein

You can be a person
who makes women happy!
Here's how.

First: Acquire an attitude. Believe you want their happiness. Say to yourself, slowly, "I want to make women happy!" Repeat it several times until you're comfortable with it. Then yell the words until they become a mantra. Repeat this mantra until your mind's eye sees happiness between you and your mom, your sister, your lover, your wife, your aunt or your friend.

How does that feel? If it doesn't click, go back to the chapter, "Feel it in Your Bones - Women Deserve Happiness," and see if you agree. If not, reread "Fixing What Is Definitely Broken."

Next: Search for a picture of yourself with a woman who is pleased to be with you. Or imagine yourself happy with a woman you know and take a self-picture. Tape the picture to the wall and focus on it daily. Memorize Dale Carnegie's words: "Picture in your mind the person you desire to be, and the thought you hold is hourly transforming you into that particular person."

Next: Envision yourself pleasing women. Relax, clear your mind, and visualize pleasing some of the women you already know. See clearly what you are doing and how they are reacting to what you are doing. Repeat the mantra, "I want to please women!"

Next: Create the future. List the women in your life whom you want to make happy.

Starting now, the person on the wall is you!

To achieve this transformation, you must want to adopt new habits. But change is about taking a risk with your ego, your way of life, your persona–a risk to be different. You are in the habit of being who you are. Being you creates an energy that gets absorbed in the molecules of your body, which are constantly replacing or refreshing older molecules. You are constantly creating the energy of being a nice guy, a victim, a person disposed to staying thin or gaining weight, a mellow person or one who argues–the energy of the person you have become.

Replace old habits with new ones.

The trick is to replace the old you with the new you. Seek support from friends and family for becoming a person who pleases women. Better yet, make a new friend who thinks the way you want to think. As time goes by, the old you will become a memory and the new you will be what actually exists.

Focusing on a vision of the future is a powerful technique for change. Bob Noyce, founder of Intel, once told me, "A vision brings the future to the present so that you can work on it right now." This way of thinking causes change. In this creative process, you consider specifically what you want the future to be and then go to work on how to achieve it. It's the kind of thinking that fulfilled John Kennedy's vision of putting human beings on the moon. Successful Silicon Valley companies have consistently demonstrated that visualizing the future, by creating a good business plan and following it passionately, produces spectacular growth rates and profitability. The business plan is a vision, a roadmap to the future. Entrepreneurs achieve fundamental change because they will their vision to happen.

If your vision is to please a woman, and you are committed, you can be that person. Why not!

Let's say, for the sake of discussion, that you have several personalities within you. I read in the papers many years ago about a case of multiple-personality in which the patient was a diabetic. When his alter ego was "out," he could eat anything without restriction and had no need for insulin. You have probably experienced situations in which you seem to change character, depending on your companions or on the circumstances. For instance, you're not the same person when you're wooing the woman of your dreams as you are after you've won her.

Start being a person who pleases women!

Step into that role right now. Remember, if you have passion for a vision, it is possible to attract or create the very personality within you that is capable of achieving that vision. Let this personality live, and let the current *you* go along for the ride. What do you have to lose, except a life of loneliness?

Becoming a man... Summary

- *Believe that you want a woman's happiness!*

- *"Picture in your mind the person you desire to be. The thought you hold is transforming you hourly into that person."* —Dale Carnegie

ATTACHMENTS

1. "Romance" Cheat Sheet *(tear out)*
Instructions: Ask what is romantic to her and write it down here. Include your own suggestions and ideas from the romance, gift or traditions sections of this book. Follow one of these ideas every three weeks. Be unpredictable.

2. Menu

This is an example of the exotic menu my friend and I prepared for our wives. Use as is or change at your discretion.

3. "Keep Her Happy" Cheat Sheet *(cut it)*
Instructions: Cut out and fold. The result will be a credit card size you can put into your wallet! If this card wears out, download another from my web site.

"Romance" Cheat Sheet

Examples:

1. Change one thing for her.
2. Start the morning off: "Good morning beautiful!"
3. Do something out of character, a spontaneous hug.
4. Clean the apartment.
5. A candle-light pasta dinner using recipe on page 20 with nice music, perhaps an Andrea Bocelli CD!
6. A bubble bath with wonderful smells!
7. E-mail or text message with simple statement of appreciation!
8. Make love in nature or against a wall, slow or wild.
9. Picnic!
10. A fun night of laughing or dancing!
11. Pretend you are strangers meeting at a designated place.

Elaborate Menu for the Advanced

Menu

En honneur de:
Malgosia et Zosia

lundi 17 Aout 1998

Chef de cuisine: Denis
Maitre de vin: Rob

Aperitif

Pinot Chardonnay
delle Venezie

Eau Minerale Evita

Apetizers

- Fromage Grenoble
- Olives Valencia
- Beets Luxembourg
- Mushrooms Kiev
- Fresh Garden Vegetables
  with sauce "Denis"

with a choice of:

Riesling (Mosel-Sagr-Ruwer) 1997

or

Bianco Villa de la Venezie

Main Course

~ Tagliatelli a la
  pomidoro, i pomidoro
  fresco Siciliano
    with
  Pain aux fromage
    gratinée
with: Chianti Cavating
        1996

Dessert

Gelatti: ~chocolate
          ~pistacio
with fresh blueberries

Digestif

~ Italian Limoncé

~ Baileys Irish Cream

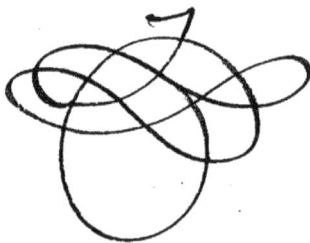

"Keep Her Happy" Cheat Sheet

IMPORTANT DATES:

Mother's Birthday ....

Mother's Day ....

Womans' Day ....

Her Mother's Bd. ....

Her Birthday: ....

Our anniversary: ....

First meeting: ....

First kiss ....

First ....

Valentine's Day: February 14th

Other ....

FLOWER RULES: 1,3,5,7...

Her favorite: ....

Anytime: Odd numbered bouquet (1, 3, 5,...). No wrapping necessary.

Romance: A single, long-stemmed red rose. A dozen roses. Flowers in season. Wrapped, with ribbon.

Special Occasion: Large bouquet. Either flowers in season or a mixed bouquet.

Can't go wrong: Bouquet of long-stemmed roses.

Get help from your local florist.

SIMPLE ANYTIME GIFTS

Non-essential cosmetics: body lotions, scented soap, fruity facial masques, etc., candles (scented or not), large, simple candle holders, colored tea-lights, incense, chocolates, bottle of wine.

Traditions! (List)

....

....

DON'T FORGET: No special occasion occasions.

SHOPPING

Sizes

Shoe:.... Waist:.... Bra:....

Underwear:.... Blouse:....

Colors

She looks good in:

She likes: ....

She doesn't like: ....

Scents she likes:..........

Favorite

Wine: ....

Chocolate: ....

Tea: ....

Flower: ....

www.ingramcontent.com/pod-product-compliance
Lightning Source LLC
Chambersburg PA
CBHW072152020426
42334CB00018B/1977